D0058538

Ellis Island

An Interactive History Adventure

by Michael Burgan

Consultant:
Zoe Burkholder, PhD
Assistant Professor, College of Education and Human Services
Montclair State University

CAPSTONE PRESS
a capstone imprint

You Choose Books are published by Capstone Press,
1710 Roe Crest Drive, North Mankato, Minnesota 56003
www.capstonepub.com

Library of Congress Cataloging-in-Publication Data
Burgan, Michael.
  Ellis Island : an interactive history adventure / by Michael Burgan.
    pages cm.—(You choose: history)
  Includes bibliographical references and index.
  ISBN 978-1-4765-0253-3 (library binding)
  ISBN 978-1-4765-3606-4 (paperback)
1. Ellis Island Immigration Station (N.Y. and N.J.)—Juvenile literature. 2. United
States—Emigration and immigration—History—Juvenile literature. I. Title.
  JV6484.B87 2014
  304.8'73—dc23   2013014256

Editorial Credits
Brenda Haugen, editor; Bobbie Nuytten, designer; Wanda Winch, media researcher;
Charmaine Whitman, production specialist

Photo Credits
Alamy: SZ Photo/Scherl, 94; Corbis: Bettmann, 50, Underwood & Underwood,
72; CriaImages.com: Jay Robert Nash Collection, 42; Library of Congress: Prints
and Photographs Division, cover, 6, 9, 19, 23, 27, 34, 47, 54, 57, 58, 67, 70, 81, 86,
91; National Archives and Records Administration (NARA), 65, ourdocuments.
gov, 83; Shutterstock: SeanPavonePhoto, 103, Songquan Deng, 100; The Statue
of Liberty-Ellis Island Foundation, Inc.,The American Immigrant Wall of Honor®,
www.wallofhonor.org, 104; YIVO Institute for Jewish Research, 12

Printed in the United States of America in Stevens Point, Wisconsin.
032013   007227WZF13

TABLE OF CONTENTS

ABOUT YOUR ADVENTURE

YOU are one of millions of immigrants who are leaving their homelands during the early 20th century to travel to the United States. When you reach America, your first stop is Ellis Island, just off the shores of New York City.

In this book you'll explore how the choices people made meant the difference between life and death. The events and work you'll experience happened to real people.

Chapter One sets the scene. Then you choose which path to read. Follow the directions at the bottom of each page. The choices you make will change your outcome. After you finish one path, go back and read the others for new perspectives and more adventures.

YOU CHOOSE the path
you take through history.

Immigrants often had few comforts on the ships that brought them to the U.S.

Coming to Ellis Island

Immigrants came to the United States long before Ellis Island opened in 1892. They came for many reasons. Some wanted to escape problems in their homelands, such as wars or famine. Some immigrants couldn't worship as they chose in Europe. Many came seeking jobs. For many, hard work led to a chance to earn more money than they could at home. Their children also had a chance to get an education.

7

Turn the page.

At times friends and family members already in the United States pulled immigrants to the country. Letters talked about the land available in the west or the jobs in factories. Most immigrants of the 19th and early 20th centuries were young men. Some came to make money and then planned to return to their homelands. Others sent for wives, children, and other relatives once they found homes and jobs.

By the 1880s many native-born white Americans were alarmed by the growing number of immigrants entering the country. Americans also noticed a change in the immigrants. Previous immigrants had come mostly from northern Europe, Germany, and the United Kingdom. Most were Protestant, which was the major faith in the United States at the time.

Ellis Island in New York was the first stop for many immigrants.

Turn the page.

But the immigrants of the 1880s and after came from southern and eastern Europe. Some were dark skinned. Many were Roman Catholic or Jewish. They spoke unfamiliar languages.

Some native-born Americans saw these new immigrants as a threat. These Americans thought the new immigrants committed crimes and spread political ideas that could weaken democracy. Some American workers also feared the immigrants would take away their jobs.

The first major law to limit immigration targeted the Chinese, who settled mostly on the west coast. That law was passed in 1882. But soon other laws affected all immigrants, including the ones entering New York City. The number of immigration laws increased after 1890.

Ellis Island will be the first stop on your search for wealth and freedom in the U.S. At Ellis Island you see the effects of the laws meant to restrict immigration. If you're lucky, you'll pass all the tests you must go through. If you're unlucky, Ellis Island might be your last stop before going back to your homeland.

→ To be a young Russian Jewish girl during the early 1900s seeking a better life in the U.S., turn to page **13**.

→ To be a teenage Italian boy landing at Ellis Island during World War I, turn to page **43**.

→ To be a German immigrant facing deportation after World War I, turn to page **73**.

A house in Russia was home to eight families and included a grocery store.

CHAPTER 2

The Trip to America

You live with your family in a part of western Russia called the Pale of Settlement. The Russian rulers set aside this area for Russian Jews long before you were born. Now, in 1909, several million Jews live there.

You ask your mother why Jews are forced to live in this region and can't travel freely in Russia.

"Because the Russians hate us," she replies. "They think we take business away from them. They think Jews are evil. That's why your father left for America. Soon we will too."

Turn the page.

Your father left your village three years ago, after a pogrom. In these vicious attacks, gangs of Russians destroyed the homes of Jews. Sometimes they killed the Jews. People in your village escaped the violence, but you have neighbors whose relatives were killed. The police did nothing to stop these brutal gangs.

You know a little about the United States from your father's letters. In one he described his voyage there and his arrival at Ellis Island. You'll go there too. But first you and your family must travel to Hamburg, Germany. From there you'll sail to New York.

You have a passport and your ticket for the ship. Mama also has money to show the officials in New York. Paupers, who are people without money, aren't allowed into the United States.

The day finally comes to begin your journey. Your heart beats fast with excitement as you stand by your mother. Next to her is your brother, Samuel, and your mother's sister, Hannah. She's going with you to meet her husband, who emigrated last year. Three large wagons wait in the village square to carry you and others to the train station.

The people jostle as they try to get into the wagons. You get separated from your family. Suddenly you hear a cry. It's Samuel! He's lying on the ground. Your mother stands over him.

Turn the page.

"What happened?" you ask after you force your way through the crowd to get to them.

"He fell, and someone stepped on him!" your mother replies, her voice thick with anger. "I think he broke his foot. He needs to see a doctor right away. Go with Hannah. We'll have to take another train. Don't worry. We'll be OK."

You want to be with your mother and brother for this long trip. But you think of the ticket in your pocket and finally seeing your father again.

➤ *To continue on with Hannah, go to page* **17**.

➤ *To stay with your mother, turn to page* **41**.

You look at your mother as you feel tears fill your eyes. "Go with Hannah," she says. "Everything will be fine."

Hannah squeezes your hand and then waves at your mother. You step into the wagon. As it pulls away, you wonder when—or if—you will see Mama and Samuel again.

The wagon takes you to the railroad station. The train is even more crowded than the wagon. People are jammed onto benches and sitting on their bags, which are crammed into the aisles. You and Hannah finally find a spot to sit.

At the German border, several men get on the train. Two of them are police officers. They stop and question everyone on board. "I think one's a doctor," your aunt says.

Turn the page.

Speaking in Russian, the doctor asks about your health. "No signs of cholera?" Hannah says no.

As the men move on, you ask Hannah, "What's cholera?"

"A sickness of the stomach. If they thought we had it and could spread it, they wouldn't let us into Germany."

You're glad you're feeling well. You would hate to turn back now.

After several days' journey on the crowded train, you finally reach Hamburg. At the docks you board the largest ship, the *Pretoria*. You enter your tiny cabin in steerage. Three levels of bunks are attached to the wall. An old woman, Leah Orloff, is already on the lowest bunk. You take the middle one. Hannah takes the top. After the ship sails, you notice your stomach feels strange. You haven't eaten much today. Maybe that's why you feel ill. Or maybe it's seasickness.

The SS *Pretoria* was used by the U.S. Navy to transport troops after World War I.

"Maybe you should see the ship's doctor," Hannah says.

You don't like doctors. But maybe he can help.

You leave the cabin and walk through the crowded ship. Your stomach feels odd, and your legs cramp a bit. When you reach the doctor, many other people are in line ahead of you. A nurse approaches. She speaks to you in a foreign language—perhaps German. You shake your head and say in Yiddish, "I don't understand."

Turn the page.

A young man behind you speaks up. "I speak Yiddish and some German. Tell me your problem, and I'll try to explain it to her."

You tell him your stomach and legs hurt. As you stand there, you feel a sudden urge to go to the bathroom. The young man points at a door. You rush to it. Later you return to the line, feeling weak.

The young man says, "The nurse says it's probably just seasickness. And maybe you're tired. Eat an apple to settle your stomach, and try to sleep."

The young man continues, "My name is Jacob. I'm from Poland. Let's see if we can find you an apple."

"But aren't you sick too?" you ask. "Why did you come to the doctor?"

"For my brother. He's in with the doctor now. Come on."

Jacob is also traveling in steerage. But he takes you to a part of the ship where the second-class passengers stay. He calls out several times in German, "Does anyone have an apple for a sick girl?" Finally a woman comes over and hands him an apple. He smiles as he hands you the fruit.

"Would you like to meet my family?" Jacob asks.

You like Jacob. It would be nice to meet his family. But Hannah is waiting for you.

➤ To go back to the cabin, turn to page **22**.

➤ To go with Jacob, turn to page **29**.

"My aunt might be worried about me," you tell Jacob. "I should go. But we can meet later."

Jacob tells you where his cabin is located. Then you turn back toward yours.

The apple didn't make you feel better. The ship is not swaying as much, but your stomach still feels upset. And you're so thirsty.

Back at the cabin, you tell Hannah what's happened. "You look awful," she says.

You feel awful too. Over the next few hours, you rush several times to a bucket that serves as a toilet.

Back in your bunk, you finally fall asleep. The next thing you know, Hannah is waking you.

"Here, drink this water."

"I'm not thirsty," you say.

"Take it," Hannah says. "And I think we should go back to the doctor."

"Find Jacob first," you say. "He can translate for us." You tell Hannah where Jacob's cabin is. You fall asleep again. When you awake, Hannah and Jacob help you to the doctor's office. The doctor looks at you while Jacob explains your symptoms. The doctor says something, and Jacob turns to you with a serious look.

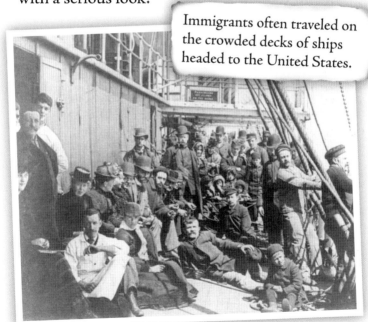

Immigrants often traveled on the crowded decks of ships headed to the United States.

Turn the page.

"He thinks you have cholera," he says. "You probably caught it before you reached Hamburg."

"What can we do?" Hannah asks.

"The doctor has some drugs here, but they don't always work," Jacob explains. "You would have to stay here in the hospital."

"I don't want to stay here!" you say. "I want to go back to the cabin with Hannah."

"But you could die!" Hannah cries.

You know that's true. But you could die if you stay at the hospital. And what if the doctor is wrong? Maybe you don't have cholera.

➤ To stay in the hospital, go to page **25**.

➤ To go with Hannah, turn to page **40**.

"I'll stay here," you say. "But tell the doctor he must let Hannah stay with me."

The doctor agrees and begins giving you the medicine. With you in the small room are other people with cholera.

Over the next week, you start feeling better. The doctor lets you return to your cabin as the ship nears New York. Finally the day comes. You and Jacob watch as the ship passes the Statue of Liberty. The deck is filled with people who want to see this symbol of hope in their new country.

When the ship docks, you board a ferry that takes you from the dock to Ellis Island. You enter a room where guards tell you to leave your things. You walk up some stairs and enter a huge hall.

Turn the page.

Many languages are being spoken as the officials question the new arrivals. Translators help the immigrants communicate. Doctors inspect you and Hannah. To check your eyes, the examiner lifts up your eyelids with a metal rod with a small hook at the end. Hannah passes through, but a translator pulls you aside.

"Your eyes don't look right," the man says. "They want to check you again." He marks your back with a piece of chalk and leads you to an examination room.

"You'll be fine," Hannah says, but she looks worried. After the doctor examines you, he speaks to the translator, who then comes over to you.

"He says you have a disease called trachoma. You have to go through another exam."

First the cholera and now this! You start to cry.

"What will happen to her?" Hannah asks.

"They will examine her again. She might have to go back to Hamburg," the man says. "And you'll have to go with her. She's too young to travel alone."

Immigrants were unloaded from a boat at Ellis Island.

Turn the page.

You're led to a room where more people examine you. A translator asks if you have money to pay for a doctor. You shake your head no.

"Then they won't let you in," the translator says. You start to cry again.

"Maybe I can get out before we sail, to tell your father," Hannah says, wiping away her own tears. "And we'll write your mother. Everything will be all right."

But you wonder what will happen as you make the long voyage back to Europe. This isn't how you had hoped your new life would turn out.

28

THE END

To follow another path, turn to page 11.
To read the conclusion, turn to page 101.

You eat the apple as you walk with Jacob. The cabins in steerage are hot, tiny, and smell of unwashed bodies. The cabins smell so bad that many people crowd outside on deck. The first- and second-class passengers are on the decks above you. They paid more money, so they have better food and nicer rooms. A few of them throw candy to the younger kids on the steerage deck. After a while you feel better. You thank Jacob for his help and go back to your cabin.

For more than a week, the ship cuts across the Atlantic. The trip is long and boring. You eat watery soup that tastes horrible. You have some of your mother's homemade bread with you, but what's left is stale. You can't wait to reach Ellis Island.

On the last night, the wind begins to howl. The seas get rough, and all around you people are moaning. Some are praying.

Turn the page.

"What's the matter?" you ask a woman.

"A storm—a terrible storm. We're right in the middle of it. The crew has never seen anything like it."

Back in the cabin, Hannah looks pale. So does the elderly woman with you, Mrs. Orloff.

"Maybe food will help," you say. "I felt better after I ate an apple."

"Oh, I don't think I could eat anything," Mrs. Orloff says. "I feel so miserable. I feel like I'm going to die."

"You won't die," Hannah says. "I'll look for food."

Maybe you should go. Hannah is sick and shouldn't be walking around the ship during a storm. But if Mrs. Orloff needed help, Hannah might not have the strength to do it.

➤ To look for food, go to page **31**.

➤ To stay in the cabin, turn to page **35**.

"I'll go," you tell Hannah. "You're too sick."

As you walk near open doors, you feel the force of the storm's wind push you. Spray shoots up from the swelling waves. Suddenly the ship rolls with tremendous force. You fly across the passageway into a wall.

"Ahhh!" you scream as you feel a sharp pain in your left arm. A crewmember helps you up. He says something in German you don't understand. You try to ignore the pain and ask in Yiddish for an apple. He leaves and quickly comes back with three apples. You put them in the pockets of your dress. Carefully, you head back to your cabin. Your arm is throbbing.

Inside the cabin Mrs. Orloff is moaning. Hannah is curled up on her bed. You hand her an apple, and she forces down a few bites. Mrs. Orloff refuses to eat.

Turn the page.

As quickly as the storm began, it ends. Hannah's seasickness gets better. You both fall asleep. Suddenly you wake up to an announcement—the ship has docked in New York! Even Mrs. Orloff looks better after hearing the news. You and Hannah gather your belongings and leave the ship. You can't wait to get on dry land.

On Ellis Island you enter a large brick building. Men in uniforms stand by, examining all the passengers. One comes over to you and checks you over. When he touches your arm, you flinch. It still hurts from your fall though you had almost forgotten about it in your excitement. He asks a question in several languages, and then says it in Yiddish.

"What happened to your arm?"

"Nothing," you say. The man takes hold of your arm and begins to move it. You yelp in pain.

"It appears to be broken," he says. "We have to take care of it."

"Hannah," you call to your aunt, "this man says I must go with him." Hannah rushes over to you. "What happened?"

The man tells her, "She'll be fine. You go through the inspection. If you pass you can see her after the doctor looks at her."

Hannah looks worried, but she nods as the men lead you to the hospital. A nurse brings you some meat and cheese inside two pieces of bread—she calls it a sandwich. You take a bite and smile. It tastes good, and you've learned your first word in English!

The doctor wraps your arm in a plaster cast. The nurse says to you in Yiddish, "The doctor wants you to stay here, just for tonight."

Turn the page.

The Statue of Liberty (top, center) was one of the first things immigrants saw as they neared New York.

You ask the nurse to find Hannah and tell her what's happening. She says Hannah is already outside the hospital. She's passed all her exams and is free to go. She will stay the night at Ellis Island. In the morning you'll see your father and begin your new life in the United States.

THE END

To follow another path, turn to page 11.
To read the conclusion, turn to page 101.

"Are you sure you're all right to go?" you ask Hannah.

"Yes, yes. Just keep an eye on Mrs. Orloff."

You lie on your bunk and hear the old woman moan. Finally she falls asleep, and you do too. When you awake, Hannah is standing by you. She's smiling.

"I never found the apples," she says. "But I feel much better. The storm is finally over. We're almost in New York!"

Even Mrs. Orloff feels better after hearing the news. You tell her good-bye as you and Hannah gather your things and go out on deck to watch the ship dock.

Turn the page.

You see Jacob and introduce him to Hannah. Jacob introduces the woman standing next to him as his mother, Sarah. Jacob explains that you'll all take ferries to Ellis Island. As the crowd moves forward, you lose sight of Hannah. Finally you see her ahead of you, waving. She's already on the first ferry.

"Hurry," she yells to you. "The boat is about to leave!"

"But there are so many people!" you shout.

"Come with us," Jacob's mother says, reaching for your hand. "You can meet your aunt on Ellis Island."

➥ To go with Jacob and Sarah, go to page **37**.

➥ To fight through the crowd and join Hannah, turn to page **39**.

"I'll be on the next boat!" you yell to Hannah. Jacob and Sarah wave to show that you're not alone, and Hannah nods.

When the next boat comes, the three of you squeeze on it. The ride to Ellis Island is short. On shore you search for Hannah. She sees you first and comes over to hug you. You say good-bye to Jacob and Sarah and thank them for their help.

You go through a series of medical exams. Then a man asks you some questions in English. Another official translates them into Yiddish.

"How much money do you have?" the official finally asks.

"I have about three dollars," you reply.

Hannah has a little more money than you do. You know plenty of Russian Jews have entered the United States with this amount of money.

Turn the page.

But the first man shakes his head. The translator says, "I'm sorry, but the rules just changed this year. The officials here expect you to have $25 dollars each to enter."

You look at Hannah and start to cry. She says to the translator, "But we have people waiting for us. They have jobs and money."

The translator replies, "You have to go to a special hearing. There officials will decide if what you say is true. Until then you have to stay here."

A woman leads you and Hannah to a detention hall. The hall is packed. Your father will need to convince the people at the hearing that what you've said is true. If he can't, you'll be sent back home, even though you're so close to realizing your dream.

THE END

To follow another path, turn to page 11.
To read the conclusion, turn to page 101.

"I have to go with Hannah," you tell Jacob and Sarah. "Good-bye, and thank you for all your help!"

You push through the crowd. Hannah is trying to get off the boat. She's going to wait for you!

On Ellis Island you go through a long line so doctors can inspect you. Then a translator helps you answer a number of questions. Finally a man says you are free to go.

At the New York dock, you search for Papa. There he is!

"Papa!" you call. He turns and sees you. You run toward each other and hug. It's so good to see him again. And you have so much to tell him about your journey to America.

THE END

To follow another path, turn to page 11.
To read the conclusion, turn to page 101.

"I'm going with Hannah," you say. "She's the only family I have here." As you leave, the doctor tells you to drink as much water as you can.

You try to follow the doctor's order. But when you drink water, you vomit it almost immediately. You fall asleep. When you wake up, you feel very weak.

"Hannah, please," you say, your voice barely a whisper. "Tell Mama and Papa I love them. And Samuel too."

"What are you saying?" Hannah asks. Your eyes slowly close. You die, never seeing Ellis Island or your new home in the United States.

THE END

To follow another path, turn to page 11.
To read the conclusion, turn to page 101.

You tell Hannah to go without you. Your mother is holding your crying brother's hand. She looks at you. "Why didn't you go with your aunt?"

"I couldn't leave without you," you say. "What if you missed the ship?"

"Silly girl," your mother says. "There will always be another. And now if we do miss the ship, your father will have to send money for three new tickets, instead of two."

You hadn't thought of that or the fact that you have sold all your belongings. You will have to find relatives who will let all three of you live with them. As the village doctor looks at Samuel's foot, you wonder if you made the right decision. You hope that you'll all still get to the U.S. before the next pogrom.

THE END

To follow another path, turn to page 11.
To read the conclusion, turn to page 101.

German troops filled the main square in Brussels, Belgium, after capturing the city in 1914.

CHAPTER 3

Life in a New Land

You are sailing on a ship that left the Spanish port of Barcelona just a few days before. It's spring 1917 and most European nations are at war. Some people call it the Great War. Your homeland, Italy, is on the side of the Allies, which include France and Great Britain. But Spain is neutral, and people can sail from there to America. The United States is not in the war—at least not yet.

43

The war has already affected your family. Your cousin Nino returned to your village from New York last year, so he could fight for Italy against Germany, the Allies' main opponent.

Turn the page.

Thousands of immigrants in America have returned to Europe during the war to fight for their homelands. Just a month after joining the Italian army, Nino was killed. Nino's father is your Uncle Tony, and you're going to America to live with him. He needs help on his farm, and your mother is afraid you'll be drafted into the military if you stay in Italy.

On the ship you met a beautiful young girl named Maria. She has relatives in America too, and she hopes to find work with them. You think you might try to convince her to stay with you in New York.

After about eight days at sea, the ship reaches New York City. Maria goes with you on the ferry to Ellis Island. But once you get there, the men and women are separated. "I'll look for you when we finish the exams," you say, and she nods.

She looks worried and hands you her address in Italy. You know some immigrants call Ellis Island "the island of tears." Even though most immigrants are allowed into the U.S., those who are turned back often cry with disappointment.

You wait in a long line. Before you reach the officials who will ask you questions, you see Maria. She's crying.

"I did not pass the literacy test," she calls out.

Literacy test! You didn't know you'd be asked to read. You left school when you were just 11 to help on the family farm. And what about Maria? You think she might make a good wife. Maybe you should flunk the test too so you can go with her. But Uncle Tony is counting on your help.

➤ To flunk the test on purpose, turn to page **46.**

➤ To try to pass the test, turn to page **48.**

Your turn finally comes. A translator tells you in Italian that you have to answer a number of questions. Did someone you don't know offer you a job in America? Have you ever been sent to prison for a crime? Are you an anarchist? You shake your head no to each question.

Finally the translator hands you a card. Half of it has words in Italian. The other half are in another language—maybe English.

"The top half is from the Bible," the man says. "Can you read it?"

You study the Italian words on the card. You won't have to pretend you can't read so you can be with Maria—you really can't! You only recognize a few words from your years at school. You look at the translator and say no.

"Then back to Italy for you," he says.

You see Maria only briefly as you're led to the detention center. You tell her what happened. "At least we can go back to Italy together," you say. "And we can come back again, when we learn how to read."

Immigrants took exams at Ellis Island.

THE END

To follow another path, turn to page 11.
To read the conclusion, turn to page 101.

You've traveled so far from home, it would be silly not to try to get into America. And your uncle needs your help. You go through all the medical exams with no problems, and a translator asks you a number of questions. He even asks you to add some numbers, and you answer correctly. Now it's time to read. The translator hands you a card with Italian words written on it. You can read it! There are a few words that you don't really understand, but you sound out all the letters and get through all 40 words.

As you get your bags and head outside, you think about Maria. You'll miss her, but maybe you'll meet again some day. And there will be lots of work on your uncle's farm to keep you busy.

You find your way to a ferry. Your uncle will meet you at the ferry docks at the southern tip of Manhattan.

When you land people bustle all around. You look for your uncle but don't see him. After a few minutes, a man approaches you. He says in Italian, "You're looking for someone?"

"Yes, my uncle. He said he would be here, but he didn't know for sure when I would arrive."

"I see," the well-dressed man says. "Yes, it happens often. That's why I come down to the ferry, to help fellow Italians. My name is Luigi Rota."

You introduce yourself, and then Luigi asks, "Where are you going?"

You explain about your uncle's farm. "I should look again for him. I'm sure he must be nearby."

Turn the page.

"Well," Luigi says, "something might have delayed him. But I can help you. Come, let's get something to eat. You must be starving."

He's right. You haven't eaten since breakfast, and your stomach is grumbling. But what if your uncle comes while you're away?

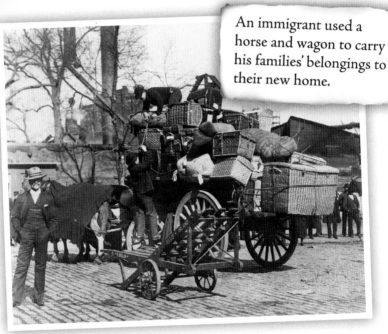

An immigrant used a horse and wagon to carry his families' belongings to their new home.

➤ *To go with Luigi, go to page 51.*

➤ *To wait for your uncle, turn to page 53.*

"I'm sure my uncle will wait for me," you tell Luigi. "Let's go find some food."

"Excellent!" Luigi says. He takes you by the arm and leads you to a stairway. "This is a subway," he says. "It's a train that goes underground."

You're amazed. The train you took to get to the port in Spain was the first one you had ever been on. Now you're going to ride on one that goes underground!

"Luigi," you ask, "how far is the restaurant? There must be plenty of places to eat around here."

"If you want the best Italian food in the city of New York, come with me."

Turn the page.

You take out some money to pay for the train. Back at Ellis Island, you exchanged all your Italian money for American dollars. You even had some gold coins that your father gave you. You're luckier than many immigrants. You have about $40 now.

Suddenly Luigi grabs the money. He pushes you down and runs to the subway. You go after him, but the hallway is packed with people. You quickly lose sight of him.

Heading back up the stairs, you feel foolish. How could you trust someone you don't know? You go back to the ferry docks. Your uncle is still not there. You slump on a bench. Tears fill your eyes as you realize that life in America might not be as easy as you thought it would be.

THE END

To follow another path, turn to page 11.
To read the conclusion, turn to page 101.

"No, thank you. I should wait for my uncle," you say. You look up and see a familiar face. "There he is now! Come on. I'll introduce you."

You run through a small crowd of people, calling Tony's name. He sees you and gives you a hug.

"Welcome to America!" he says.

You tell him all about Maria and the literacy test at Ellis Island. Then you tell Tony you want him to meet Luigi. But Luigi is nowhere to be seen.

"Good thing," Tony says when you tell him what happened. "He probably just wanted to rob a greenhorn."

"Greenhorn?" you ask, confused.

"Somebody just off the boat from Europe who doesn't know who to trust," Tony answers. "Somebody like you."

Turn the page.

Tony buys you a hot sandwich from a pushcart vendor. Then he leads you to a train that will take you to his farm. He tells you his farm is in a place called Oswego. "It's far," he explains. "It's about 300 miles away. But it's beautiful."

After crossing the Atlantic, 300 miles doesn't seem so far. Tony tells you that the train can reach speeds of 80 miles per hour—much faster than the train you rode to the port in Spain.

Industry grew along the waterways in Oswego, New York.

You settle in on your uncle's farm. It's a small orchard where he grows apples and pears. He explains that he doesn't make enough money selling fruit. Sometimes he works at other jobs around town. "I might help build a road or cut down trees," he says. "Lots of Italians here do that kind of work."

Over the next few weeks, you help your uncle and do odd jobs in town. You still sometimes think about Maria. You ask Tony to help you write a letter to her. You receive a letter back that Maria's sister wrote for her. She says Maria misses you! Maybe you should go back to Italy to help her learn to read. Then you can come back together to New York. But Tony is counting on your help.

➻ *To go back to Italy, turn to page **56**.*

➻ *To stay in Oswego, turn to page **66**.*

You tell your uncle about the letter and your decision to go back to Italy. You're afraid he'll be angry, but instead he smiles.

"If you want to be with Maria, you should go. Soon enough your younger cousins will be old enough to help more."

You hug your uncle. But now you have another problem—paying for your trip.

"You need a real job," Tony says. "Not these odd jobs you've been doing. Let me talk to someone down at the factory."

You know he means the match factory. It's one of the places in Oswego that will hire Italians.

Oswego is located by Lake Ontario in the north-central part of New York.

The next day your uncle has good news. His friend at the match factory has a job for you! You learn how to run a machine that makes wooden matches. You work many hours every day, but it's easier than building roads. You write Maria to tell her about your plan to return to Italy to be with her.

Turn the page.

The United States used posters to encourage men to volunteer to fight during World War I.

One April morning, your uncle comes into your room with a newspaper. It's printed in New York City, but it's written in Italian. Many immigrant communities in the United States have their own newspapers.

"The United States is going to war!" Tony exclaims. "The Germans have been attacking U.S. ships, and Congress has declared war."

"What does that mean?" you ask.

"It means you could get drafted eventually and get sent to France. Do you want to fight for America?"

"What else could I do?" you ask.

"We have cousins in Argentina. You could go there and keep working until the war is over."

Argentina! That means another long sea voyage. Maybe you should just stay in Oswego and hope you don't get drafted. But if you get drafted, you might never make it back to Italy to see Maria.

→ To go to Argentina, turn to page **60**.

→ To stay in Oswego, turn to page **61**.

Your uncle writes to the cousins in Argentina. You keep working at the match factory and help around the orchard when you can. The United States hasn't started a draft yet. But you learn that on June 5, 1917, many young men, even immigrants, must register for the draft. You're too young to register now, but who knows what will happen if the war goes on?

Finally you hear from the relatives in Argentina. Even though they've never met you, they will welcome you. With some money from Tony, you buy a ticket on a ship sailing from New York.

You thank Tony and then head to the docks of New York City. Your ship sails past the Statue of Liberty and Ellis Island. You hope that one day you and Maria can return to the United States for good.

THE END

To follow another path, turn to page 11.
To read the conclusion, turn to page 101.

"I should keep working and save my money," you tell Tony. "Maybe there won't be a draft after all."

A few weeks later, though, Tony reads in the paper that the United States will begin drafting young men. "But you don't have to worry," he says. You're still too young." He explains that only men between 21 and 31 have to register.

At the match factory, some of the Italian workers talk about the war. A man named Carlo says, "I hear if you volunteer for the Army, you can become a U.S. citizen."

"No, no," another man says. "It's not true. You can volunteer if you want, but they won't make you a citizen."

Turn the page.

At home that night, you ask your uncle if he's heard about immigrants becoming citizens if they fight. "Some guys around town say so," Tony tells you. "But people say a lot of things."

The next day, you ask Carlo if he's going to volunteer for the Army.

"Today," he says. "What about you? Don't you want to be a citizen?"

If Carlo's right you can join the Army and become a U.S. citizen. If you marry Maria, it would then be easier to get her into the country. But if he's wrong, you could be taking a risk for nothing.

➤ To stay at the factory, go to page **63**.

➤ To go with Carlo to volunteer, turn to page **64**.

"I don't want to be a soldier," you tell Carlo. "I'm going to keep working and save my money."

As the war goes on, you spend nights taking English classes. You're a good student. Picking up a newspaper, you see that Carlo was wrong. Immigrants aren't made citizens if they fight in the war. You're glad you decided to stay in Oswego.

But as the war in Europe drags on, the U.S. needs more soldiers. The government changes the draft law. Now that you've turned 18, you have to register for the draft. But you are in luck! On November 11, 1918, the war ends! And you receive a letter from Maria with more good news. She is coming to the U.S. again! You make plans to go back to Ellis Island—this time to welcome Maria as she joins you in New York.

63

THE END

To follow another path, turn to page 11.
To read the conclusion, turn to page 101.

You and Carlo walk to the local draft board. The man at the desk gives you papers to fill out. A doctor gives you several medical tests, which you pass.

In September 1917 you arrive at Camp Upton on Long Island. It's almost like being at Ellis Island again. Many of the new soldiers are immigrants, and they speak many languages. Many, like you, know barely any English. You go through months of training. You learn how to fire a gun and about mustard gas, a dangerous chemical.

While you're in camp, you learn that Carlo was wrong. You won't become a U.S. citizen just for enlisting. But there's talk the government will change the law and make you a citizen later.

Finally you and the other men in your division get news that you're going to France. After another long voyage across the Atlantic Ocean, you head to the front, where the fighting takes place.

Your sergeant orders you to attack a German line. You rise from your trench, your rifle in hand. Boom! A bullet from an enemy gun hits you in the chest. You die on the fields of France, along with so many others during this long, bloody war.

U.S. troops battled the Germans in 1918.

THE END

To follow another path, turn to page 11.
To read the conclusion, turn to page 101.

You tell Tony about Maria's feelings. "But I want to stay here and earn money," you say. "Then I'll bring Maria here."

Tony likes your decision and how hard you work. But one day in April he comes into your room, frowning.

"I just heard the news. America is at war with Germany."

"Will you have to fight?" you ask.

"I'm too old. And you're too young. But other Italians here, they might have to go. President Wilson wants to draft men into the military."

When you go into town, you hear about fellow Italians who will be going to war. Some had already joined the National Guard. After June 1917 some are drafted. And others decide to volunteer. Perhaps you should volunteer too. You talk to Tony about your idea.

President Woodrow Wilson asked Congress to declare war on Germany on April 2, 1917.

"Why do you want to do that?" he asks.

"America is my country now," you say. "And the president says it's a war for freedom. Everybody should have freedom."

"But you could get killed, like my son Nino! And what about Maria?"

Of course—Maria! What about her and your plans for marriage? But you want to support your new country.

→To stay in Oswego, turn to page 68.

→To volunteer for the Army, turn to page 69.

"I'll stay, Tony," you say. "For Maria. And you."

As the months go on, you take classes in town to learn English. You read the newspaper to learn about the war. You read in 1918 that the government wants men your age to register for the draft. You register, but you're one of the lucky ones who are never called to serve. On November 11, 1918, you hear wonderful news—the war is over! Soon soldiers begin returning to Oswego from Europe.

One day that winter, you begin to feel a little sick. You think it's a cold, but soon you're in bed with a high fever. Your body is weak. The doctor says you have influenza. The disease has been spreading quickly around the country, killing many people. You die three days later. You missed the war, but death came for you anyway.

THE END

To follow another path, turn to page 11.
To read the conclusion, turn to page 101.

You go to the local draft board the next day and pass all the tests. You take a train with other soldiers to South Carolina, where you begin months of training.

The weather is warm there, like in Italy. But in Italy you never marched with a 70-pound pack on your back. You also hear some of the Americans call you and the other Italians names such as "Wop" and "Dago." Some of the Italians start fights when they hear these insults. You just keep quiet and do what you're told.

In May 1918 your division begins the long trip to France. That's where most of the fighting is taking place. Weeks pass before you see any action, but now you're under heavy fire from the Germans.

Turn the page.

Taking cover in a trench, you hear enemy machine guns firing all around. But the men around you are not fighting back, since they can't get a clear shot. When one bullet strikes your friend Giovanni, you jump out of the ditch. Joe, another Italian American, follows you.

U.S. soldiers advanced in their attack along the River Somme in northern France.

With bullets whizzing by, you fire at the German machine gunners who are hiding in a trench. When you run out of bullets, you and Joe throw grenades. You feel a bullet rip into your arm, but you keep advancing. You jump into a German trench, and the soldiers inside put up their arms and surrender. You and Joe return to your line with 21 prisoners.

Your sergeant says, "That was pretty crazy, what you did. And brave."

You smile. It feels good to be a hero fighting for your new country. And once your arm is bandaged, you'll be ready to fight again.

71

THE END

To follow another path, turn to page 11.
To read the conclusion, turn to page 101.

Immigrants waited in long lines in the registration room on Ellis Island.

CHAPTER 4

Questions of Loyalty

It's 1919, and the Great War is over. You're happy for the Allies' victory, and for German-Americans too. You, like many others, were a victim of hatred during the war.

When your family landed at Ellis Island 15 years ago, the officials changed your family's last name. Messerschmidt became Smith. But your parents didn't care. They were just glad to be in the United States. You settled in a part of Manhattan where many Germans live—Klein Deutschland, which means "Little Germany."

73

Turn the page.

Since then you've worked hard to become an American. You went to school for a few years and learned to speak English. Two years ago you got a job at a meatpacking plant. Nobody bothered you there—until the United States entered the war.

Millions of Americans began to hate anything German. Some schools stopped teaching the language. Books written in German were taken out of many libraries. You told everyone that you were American now, not German. Before the war you had begun the process of becoming a U.S. citizen.

With the war over, you hope all the anti-German feelings will stop. Besides, the country has new problems. Prices are rising, and many returning soldiers can't find jobs. Outside work one afternoon, you hear some of the men talking about socialism and anarchism.

"What are those?" you ask John, an immigrant from Russia. He seems to know plenty about politics and the economy.

"They're forms of government that help working men like you and me have more money," John says. "You should come to a meeting I'm going to after work."

You're not rich, but you have everything you need. You know that at Ellis Island, anarchists aren't allowed into the country. There must be something dangerous about them. Still, you're curious about John's ideas.

➤ To refuse John's invitation, turn to page **76**.

➤ To go with John to the meeting, turn to page **78**.

"No, that's all right," you tell John. "I can always go the library to learn more about them."

"That's too bad," John says. "We need all the support we can get."

As you walk to the bus for the ride home, you notice a man in a jacket and tie approaching you. He calls your name, and you stop.

"What is it?" you ask.

He pulls out a badge. "I'm Agent Richard Jennings. I work for the Bureau of Investigation. Ever hear of it?"

You shake your head no.

"We're keeping an eye out for troublemakers —anarchists and socialists who want to hurt the country. Like your friend John at the plant."

"John talks a lot," you say, "but he wouldn't hurt anyone."

"Maybe, maybe not," the agent says. "That's what we want you to find out. We want you to be an informant." He explains that the BI will pay you to go to the meetings John attends and join any political groups he joins. Then you'll report on everything you learn.

You could use extra money. And you like the idea of helping your country. But John is a friend. It feels wrong to spy on him.

➥ *To say no, turn to page* **97.**

➥ *To say yes, turn to page* **98.**

That night John takes you to a hall not far from Little Germany. As you enter, a man hands you a newspaper written in German. Many of the headlines mention socialism and capitalism. You ask John what capitalism is.

"It's what we have here in America," he says. "Rich people own all the businesses. We say the workers should own the businesses!"

The speakers that night say the same thing. They say socialism offers a better way for immigrants. The workers might have to fight to bring about socialism.

"There was a revolution in Russia just two years ago," one speaker says. "It brought in a version of socialism. Maybe we need a revolution here too!"

After the last speaker, John turns to you. "Well, what do you think? Do you want to become a socialist and help us build a better country?"

You like the idea of improving working conditions for everyone. But why shouldn't one person be allowed to own a business and do the best he can for himself? You'd like to open your own butcher shop someday. You wouldn't want your workers taking over the business from you.

➤ *To become a socialist, turn to page **80**.*

➤ *To refuse to become a socialist, turn to page **89**.*

"I'm not sure I agree with everything I heard tonight," you tell John. "But I want to learn more. I'll go with you to more meetings."

John introduces you to his friends from Russia. They explain more about socialism. Some talk about anarchism too. You also meet men from a radical union called the Industrial Workers of the World. The members are called Wobblies. They talk about how horrible the Great War was.

"We'll never have peace as long as millions of people struggle to live, while the rich have everything they want," one Wobbly says.

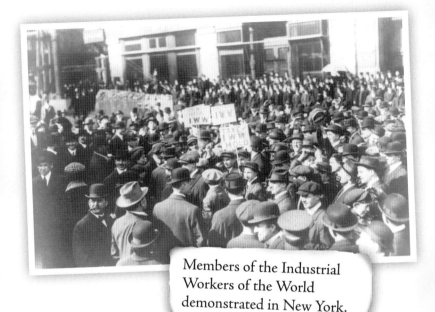

Members of the Industrial
Workers of the World
demonstrated in New York.

You begin to agree more with the socialists
and the Wobblies. You know many men who
work long hours for little pay. You go to more
meetings and tell your friends in Little Germany
about socialism. One, Kurt, gets angry with you.

Turn the page.

"This country has been good to me and you," he says. "We have freedom. We have jobs."

"But things could be better," you say.

"Go away," Kurt says. "Many people think all immigrants are radicals. I don't want anyone to think I believe in that garbage."

One night during the summer of 1919, you're attending another meeting of anarchists and socialists. Suddenly a team of men with guns storms inside. One man shouts, "We're from the Bureau of Investigation. You're under arrest for breaking the Sedition Act!"

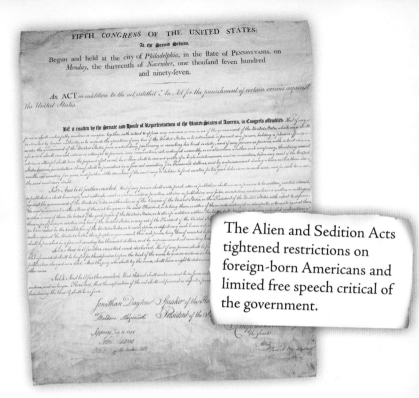

The Alien and Sedition Acts tightened restrictions on foreign-born Americans and limited free speech critical of the government.

The people in the room begin to panic. Most, like you, are immigrants who are not citizens yet. You could be deported for breaking the law. A few men run. You wonder if you should join them. But if you run, the BI men might think you're a criminal.

⇀ To run, turn to page 84.

⇀ To stay, turn to page 87.

The BI agents already think you've broken the law just by being at the meeting. You might as well run. You go through a side door that leads into an alley. You turn left and come out on the main street. More BI men and police are outside the hall. One of them spots you.

"Hold it!" an officer yells, his gun in hand. You put up your hands, and he takes you to jail. A ferry takes you from Manhattan to Ellis Island. You're led into a cell. A week later, you're in front of officials who will decide whether you can stay in the United States.

"You attended many meetings with anarchists and socialists," one official says.

"Yes, I did. But I don't believe in violence. I just want to make America better," you say.

"You paid dues to an organization that believes in violence," another official says. "We have a record of that."

You do remember giving a few dollars once to a friend of John's. You didn't know that made you a member of an anarchist group. You explain that to the officials.

"It doesn't matter," one says. "You gave money, so you belonged. That's grounds for deportation."

Turn the page.

Immigrants labeled as undesirable waited to be sent back to their homelands.

A guard takes you back to your cell. When you first came to Ellis Island, you thought you were going to build a great life in the United States. Now you wait to be sent back to Germany. Your parents will be so disappointed in you.

THE END

To follow another path, turn to page 11.
To read the conclusion, turn to page 101.

You don't resist as a police officer roughly handcuffs you. The police take you to Ellis Island. There the government will decide whether to deport you.

You go before a group of men called the Board of Inquiry. They ask you many questions about the meetings you attended. You explain that you just wanted to learn more about socialism, but that's all. Still the men say you must be deported.

Ed, another prisoner at Ellis Island, has a lawyer who is helping him. You tell the lawyer, Herb Wilson, about your case.

Turn the page.

"You have one more thing you can do to avoid deportation," Wilson says. "You can appeal the decision to the Department of Labor." He explains that the department is part of the federal government. The lawyer helps you prepare the appeal, which goes to Washington, D.C.

One day, as you sit in your cell, a guard approaches. "Smith, get up," he says. He leads you to one of the men from the Board of Inquiry. "We just heard from Washington," he says. "You've won your appeal. You're free to go."

You jump in the air with your hands raised. You know you're no danger to the United States. You board a ferry leaving Ellis Island a second time and promise yourself to stay away from John and his radical friends.

THE END

To follow another path, turn to page 11.
To read the conclusion, turn to page 101.

"I don't like all this talk about revolution," you say. "I just want to do my job and live in peace."

As you leave the meeting hall, you see a group of police officers coming up the street. They stop all the men leaving the hall, including you.

"Are you an anarchist?" the officer asks angrily. "We saw you coming out of that meeting. Do you believe in organized government?"

You're both scared and confused. "I don't know," you say.

The officer grabs you and throws you in a police truck. You and several other men who were at the meeting are put in jail. There you're allowed to make one phone call. You call your uncle Gustav, the only person you know with a phone.

Turn the page.

"Don't worry," your uncle tells you. "We'll find some money and hire a lawyer. You'll be all right."

That night you hear some of the men talking in German. They're trying to figure out how they can escape before the officers take you to Ellis Island. It serves as a prison for immigrants who are considered dangerous.

The men talk about ganging up on the guards when they take you out of the cell. One of the men, Friedrich, asks if you speak German. You nod.

"Do you want to help us?"

You don't know if their plan will work. If it doesn't you might be deported. What if your uncle can't find money for a lawyer?

→ To join the men, go to page 91.

→ To refuse, turn to page 93.

"Yes," you say. "I'll help. I don't want to go to Ellis Island."

The cell is now crowded with men arrested at the meeting hall. You recognize Hans, another immigrant from the plant. He has been listening to the men talk about their plans. After a few minutes, Hans goes to a guard standing just outside the cell. You see him whisper something to the guard. A few minutes later, several officers come into the cell.

In good weather immigrants were held in a detention pen on the roof of the main building at Ellis Island.

Turn the page.

Hans points at several of the men who have been planning the escape. He must be an informant. He's actually working for the government! Hans looks at you and raises his hand, but he doesn't point. Your body goes weak with relief. You realize Hans has told the officers about the plan. They are going to remove everyone who was going to try to escape.

The officers handcuff all the men Hans pointed at. He leaves with them too. You wonder why you were so foolish to think you could escape. You try to sleep, knowing that in the morning you'll be going to Ellis Island. You hope your uncle can find a lawyer, and you can prove you're not working against the U.S. government.

THE END

To follow another path, turn to page 11.
To read the conclusion, turn to page 101.

"You're crazy," you tell Friedrich. "You'll never get out of here."

Friedrich looks at you with disgust. You find a small space on the floor where you can get some sleep.

The next morning you board a ferry to Ellis Island. You enter a part of the building you didn't see the first time you were here. The halls are dark and cold. Other prisoners are already there. Some look as if they're barely teenagers.

As the days pass, you learn that immigrants from all over the United States have been sent here. They have been accused of being threats to the government. You meet one of them. His name is Alexander Berkman.

"I am an anarchist," Berkman says, "and proud of it. What about you?"

Turn the page.

"I'm an American who just wants to live in peace," you say. "I'm no anarchist or socialist."

"Too bad," Berkman says. The next day he is one of 249 people sent back to Russia.

A number of rejected immigrants were forced to leave the United States.

Finally your uncle Gustav comes to visit with a lawyer, Henry Wheeler. A guard watches as you talk to them from behind a metal screen.

"Your hearing is tomorrow," Wheeler says. "We'll argue that you're not too smart. You didn't know what you were doing when you went to the meeting. Will you go along with that?"

You feel a little angry. He wants you to pretend to be stupid! You know that's not true. But it might be your only chance of going back to Manhattan.

You go to the hearing the next day. You listen as Wheeler explains that you didn't have much schooling and didn't understand what the socialists were doing.

Turn the page.

One board member asks, "Did you know what was going on in that meeting?"

You shake your head.

"And you're not an anarchist or socialist?"

"No!" you exclaim.

When the hearing is over, you go back to your room. You feel your stomach tighten as you wonder what the board will decide. Finally Wheeler comes to see you.

He smiles. "You're free!"

You hug Wheeler. Playing dumb turned out to be a smart thing to do. Now you can go back home and save your money for that butcher shop.

THE END

To follow another path, turn to page 11.
To read the conclusion, turn to page 101.

"I'm sorry, sir," you say. "I don't know anything bad about John. All he's doing is talking. We have free speech in America, yes?"

"Sometimes speech leads to action," Jennings says. "And these anarchists and socialists, most of them are foreigners. We can't trust them. We'll see if I'm right about your friend."

During the next few weeks, you see John talking to other workers. Then he's gone. A friend tells you John went to Canada.

When you ask why, the man draws closer and whispers. "I think the police were after him. Some of the men here say he was an anarchist."

You hope John stays in Canada so he can't spread his radical ideas in the United States.

THE END

To follow another path, turn to page 11.
To read the conclusion, turn to page 101.

Over the next few weeks, you go to several meetings with John. The men talk about giving workers more power to control the factories and the government. No one mentions anarchists or violence. But then, after one meeting, John introduces you to some Russian immigrants who also work at the plant.

"The time has come to act," John says. "We can't just talk about changing the government. We are going to plant bombs here in New York and in other cities. Will you help?"

Killing people with bombs! You thought John wanted to help workers. Now you see that he is an anarchist—a deadly one.

"Yes, I'll help," you tell John. But as soon as you leave the meeting, you find a pay phone and call Jennings. You explain to him about the bomb plot.

"Good work," Jennings says. "We'll take care of it."

The next day a team of police officers swarms into the plant. They round up John and his friends. That evening you meet with Jennings.

"What will happen to them?" you ask.

"They'll go to trial," he says. "If they're found guilty, we'll ship them back to Russia. Thanks again for your help."

You smile, glad to know that the BI stopped John before he could harm anyone.

99

THE END

To follow another path, turn to page 11.
To read the conclusion, turn to page 101.

Visitors toured the Ellis Island Museum and learned more about U.S. immigration.

CHAPTER 5

Ellis Island Today

After World War I immigrants again came to the United States in large numbers, although not like before the war. New laws passed during the 1920s played a part, restricting the number of people who could enter the United States. The laws especially targeted the "new" immigrants of southern and eastern Europe. Ellis Island remained open, but it would never see the millions of immigrants it once did.

Another change reduced the island's role in screening newcomers. U.S. officials in Europe began processing immigrants. These officials performed the medical tests and asked the questions workers at Ellis Island once did.

In the 1930s Ellis Island served as a prison for immigrants waiting to be deported, as it did after World War I. During World War II, it also housed enemy aliens—immigrants from the countries the United States battled during the war. Most came from Germany and Italy, though some Japanese were held there too.

Ellis Island served as a prison for immigrants facing deportation until 1954. For years the building that once was filled with the voices of immigrants from many lands fell silent. The U.S. government tried but failed to sell the island. In 1965 the National Park Service was put in charge of Ellis Island.

During the 1980s the government decided to repair the crumbling buildings at Ellis Island and turn the site into a museum. Today the restored Ellis Island reminds all Americans about the millions of immigrants who entered the country there. The museum also explains how the country tried to keep out some immigrants. And people can do research there about family members who passed through Ellis Island.

Luggage left by some of the immigrants is on display at the Ellis Island Museum.

Many Americans have paid money to have their parents' or grandparents' names carved into the Wall of Honor outside the museum. More than 700,000 names are on the wall. These include immigrants who entered the U.S. at any port, not just New York.

Visitors look at the names on the Wall of Honor.

Immigration is an important part of American history. Ellis Island played a huge role. For millions of people, Ellis Island was the first stop on the way to a new life. For some others it was their last stop before being forced back to their homelands. Today it stands as a symbol of the hope the United States offers all of its citizens.

Timeline

1882—First major law designed to limit immigration is directed toward the Chinese.

1892—The first immigration facilities on Ellis Island open.

1903–1906—Many Russian Jews come to the U.S. to escape pogroms.

1909—Ellis Island officials are allowed to refuse entry to immigrants who arrive with less than $25.

1914—World War I begins in Europe; some immigrants in the U.S. return to fight for their homelands.

1917—The U.S. government requires immigrants to pass a literacy test; the United States enters World War I; immigrants and other young men are required to register for the draft.

1918—World War I ends; the world faces a worldwide outbreak of influenza that kills millions of people.

1919—The U.S. government begins searching for radicals, mostly immigrants, thought to be a danger to the country; hundreds of them are deported.

1921—Congress passes a law designed to limit European immigration.

1924—A second immigration law further reduces the number of immigrants from southern, central, and eastern Europe.

1940s—Ellis Island serves as a prison for enemy aliens and other immigrants facing deportation.

1954—Ellis Island's immigration offices close.

1965—The National Park Service is put in charge of Ellis Island.

1990—The main building on Ellis Island opens as a museum devoted to the immigrant experience there.

2001—The American Family Immigration History Center opens; visitors to the center and its website, *www.ellisisland.org*, can explore a huge collection of passenger records.

OTHER PATHS TO EXPLORE

In this book you've seen how events from the past look different from three points of view. Perspectives on history are as varied as the people who lived it. Here are ideas for other Ellis Island points of view to explore.

+ Imagine that you are a guard at Ellis Island during the peak years of immigration from Europe. Your actions can help the immigrants or make their lives miserable. Using details in the text, describe one thing you might have done to help an immigrant and something else you might have done to make the life of an immigrant miserable. (Common Core: Key Ideas and Details)

+ Many of the immigrants to Ellis Island were children. Describe what happened to children who were ill when they arrived. Many of these children did not speak English. Describe how being in a hospital alone might have made living in a new country even more challenging than if a child had arrived healthy. (Common Core: Integration of Knowledge and Ideas)

READ MORE

Benoit, Peter. *Immigration.* New York: Children's Press, 2012.

Bial, Raymond. *Ellis Island: Coming to the Land of Liberty.* Boston: Houghton Mifflin Books for Children, 2009.

Raum, Elizabeth. *German Immigrants in America: An Interactive History.* Mankato, Minn: Capstone Press, 2008.

Swain, Gwenyth. *Hope and Tears: Ellis Island Voices.* Honesdale, Penn.: Calkins Creek, 2012.

INTERNET SITES

Use FactHound to find Internet sites related to this book. All of the sites on FactHound have been researched by our staff.

Here's all you do:
Visit *www.facthound.com*
Type in this code: 9781476502533

Glossary

Allies (AL-eyz)—a group of countries that fought together in World War I; the Allies included the United States, Great Britain, France, and Italy

anarchist (AN-ahr-kist)—a person who believes in a social system that calls for ending government and having people solve their problems as a group without elected leadership

capitalism (KAP-uh-tuh-liz-uhm)—an economic system that allows people to freely create businesses and own as much property as they can afford

economy (i-KAH-nuh-mee)—the way a country produces, distributes, and uses its money, natural resources, and services

famine (FA-muhn)—a serious shortage of food resulting in widespread hunger and death

immigrate (IM-uh-grayt)—to come from a country to live in another country permanently

literacy (LIT-ur-uh-see)—the ability to read and write

neutral (NOO-truhl)—not taking sides

pogrom (POH-gruhm)—an organized attack against a minority group, particularly Jewish people

radical (RAD-i-kuhl)—extreme compared to what most people think or do

socialism (SOH-shuh-li-zuhm)—an economic system in which the goods made by factories, businesses, and farms are controlled by the government

steerage (STEER-udg)—the least expensive section of a ship for passengers

BIBLIOGRAPHY

American Experience. *"Emma Goldman."* 29 May 2013. www.pbs.org/wgbh/amex/goldman/filmmore/pt.html

Antin, Mary. *The Promised Land.* Boston: Houghton Mifflin, 1969.

Cannato, Vincent J. *American Passage: The History of Ellis Island.* New York: Harper, 2009.

Coan, Peter Morton. *Ellis Island Interviews: In Their Own Words.* New York: Facts on File, 1997.

Daniels, Roger. *Coming to America: A History of Immigration and Ethnicity in American Life.* New York: Perennial, 2002.

Iorizzo, Luciano J. *"The Impact of World War I and World War II on Italian Americans in Oswego, New York: A Preliminary View."* Oswego Historian. 29 May 2013. http://oswegohistorian.org/2011/07/impact-world-war-1-and-world-war-2-italian-americans-oswego-new-york/

La Sorte, Michael. *La Merica: Images of Italian Greenhorn Experience.* Philadelphia: Temple University Press, 1985.

Laskin, David. *The Long Way Home: An American Journey From Ellis Island to the Great War.* New York: Harper, 2010.

Morrison, Joan, and Charlotte Fox Zabusky. *American Mosaic: The Immigrant Experience in the Words of Those Who Lived It.* New York: E. P. Dutton, 1980.

Schmidt, Regin. *Red Scare: FBI and the Origins of Anticommunism in the United States, 1919-1943.* Copenhagen: Museum Tusculanum Press, 2000.

Yans-McLaughlin, Virginia, and Marjorie Lightman. *Ellis Island and the Peopling of America: The Official Guide.* New York: New Press, 1997.

INDEX